Secrets Unveiled: Stories of Great Spies and Their Impact on History

ROBERTO MIGUEL RODRIGUEZ

Copyright Page

TITLE: Secrets Unveiled: Stories of Great Spies and Their Impact on History

1ST Edition

Copyright @ 2023

ISBN: 9798223920373

Table of Contents

Secrets Unveiled: Stories of Great Spies and Their Impact on History

By Roberto Miguel Rodriguez

Chapter 1: The Birth of Espionage

The Origins of Spying in Ancient Civilizations

In the subchapter titled "The Origins of Spying in Ancient Civilizations," we delve into the intriguing history of espionage and its roots in ancient times. This chapter aims to captivate historians by exploring the early practices of spying, shedding light on the fascinating stories that shaped the world of intelligence gathering.

Throughout human history, civilizations have recognized the importance of acquiring information about their adversaries, leading to the birth of espionage. Our journey begins with tales of spies who operated in ancient civilizations such as Egypt, Mesopotamia, and China. These early spies played a crucial role in shaping the events of their time and contributed significantly to the course of history.

Within these pages, readers will uncover stories of double agents and their impact on espionage. We explore the intricate webs of deception spun by these spies, who skillfully infiltrated enemy organizations, gathering critical intelligence that often proved instrumental in shaping the outcome of wars and conflicts.

Furthermore, we recount the tales of covert operatives and their successful missions. From ancient Greece to the Byzantine Empire, these spies risked their lives to protect their respective nations, often going undercover and adopting new identities to carry out their missions undetected. Their dedication and bravery forever left an indelible mark on the annals of history.

But not all stories told here are tales of triumph. We also explore the consequences faced by spies who were ultimately betrayed. These accounts shed light on the risks inherent in the world of espionage and the grave repercussions that awaited those unfortunate enough to be exposed.

Additionally, we delve into the stories of spies who turned against their own agencies, causing significant damage in the process. These accounts reveal the dark side of intelligence gathering, where loyalty can be easily swayed and the consequences can be dire.

Finally, we turn our attention to the modern era, where spies operate in the cyber realm, shaping the landscape of modern warfare. These stories highlight the impact of technological advancements on intelligence gathering and the challenges faced by spies in the digital age.

"The Origins of Spying in Ancient Civilizations" offers historians a captivating journey through the clandestine world of espionage. From ancient times to the present day, the stories within these pages provide a comprehensive understanding of the significant contributions and damages made by great spies throughout history.

Spies in Early Warfare: From Sun Tzu to Julius Caesar

Throughout history, the use of spies has played a vital role in shaping the outcome of wars and influencing the course of history. From ancient times to the rise of powerful empires, the art of espionage has been a powerful tool in the hands of military strategists and political leaders. In this subchapter, we explore the fascinating stories of great spies and their impact on early warfare, specifically focusing on the influential figures from Sun Tzu to Julius Caesar.

Sun Tzu, the renowned ancient Chinese military strategist, recognized the importance of intelligence gathering in warfare. His famous treatise, "The Art of War," emphasized the significance of spies as a means to gain valuable information about the enemy's strengths, weaknesses, and intentions. Sun Tzu's teachings served as a foundation for future generations of spies and their contribution to military success.

Moving westward, we delve into the world of ancient Rome and the formidable figure of Julius Caesar. Caesar's military brilliance was complemented by his skillful use of spies. He employed a vast network of informants to infiltrate enemy organizations and gather critical intelligence. Caesar's spies played a pivotal role in identifying potential threats, uncovering enemy strategies, and ensuring the success of his military campaigns.

These early examples of espionage highlight the significant influence spies had on the outcome of wars. Their success or failure often determined the fate of nations and shaped the course of history. From double agents who worked undercover, risking their lives for their countries, to female spies who made significant contributions in a male-dominated world, the stories of these individuals captivate our imagination and shed light on the intricacies of espionage.

However, not all spies were successful in their endeavors. Betrayal was always a lurking danger, and those who were ultimately betrayed faced severe consequences. The impact of spies who turned against their own agencies and caused damage cannot be underestimated. Their actions not only compromised national security but also had far-reaching implications for global affairs.

As we explore the realm of early warfare espionage, it is essential to recognize the evolution of spying techniques and their adaptation to modern warfare. From the cyber realm to high-level political espionage, the role of spies continues to shape the world we live in today.

In "Secrets Unveiled: Stories of Great Spies and Their Impact on History," we invite historians to delve into the captivating tales of spies in early warfare. Through these accounts, we gain a deeper understanding of the world of espionage, its successes, failures, and the profound influence it has had on the course of human history.

The Role of Spies in Medieval Times

In the annals of history, the era of medieval times stands out as a time of great intrigue and mystery. It was a period when empires clashed, kingdoms rose and fell, and power shifted like the tides. Amidst this chaos, a shadowy group of individuals played a pivotal role in shaping the course of events – spies.

Spies in medieval times were the unsung heroes and villains of their age. They operated in the shadows, gathering critical intelligence and performing covert operations that often determined the outcome of wars and the fate of nations. Their stories are filled with tales of bravery, treachery, and sacrifice.

One of the most famous spies of the medieval era was William Marshal, a knight who served as a double agent during the Hundred Years' War. Marshal infiltrated enemy organizations, gathering vital information and relaying it to his superiors. His actions played a crucial role in turning the tide of the war in favor of his own kingdom.

But not all spies had noble intentions. The infamous spy, Elspeth MacLeod, was a master of deception and manipulation. She seduced powerful men in enemy territories, gathering sensitive information and using it to her advantage. MacLeod's actions caused chaos and confusion, ultimately leading to the downfall of several kingdoms.

The role of spies during wartime cannot be overstated. They risked their lives going undercover, infiltrating enemy lines, and gathering intelligence on enemy movements. These brave individuals operated in the shadows, often facing severe consequences if discovered. Their actions, however, saved countless lives and shaped the course of history.

Even women played a significant role in medieval espionage. Joan of Arc, the legendary French heroine, not only led armies on the battlefield but also acted as a spy, gathering critical information to aid her cause. Her contributions were instrumental in the success of the French resistance against English occupation.

The medieval era was also marked by spies who ultimately faced betrayal and its dire consequences. The story of Guy Fawkes, the infamous gunpowder plotter, serves as a cautionary tale of the dangers faced by spies. Fawkes was ultimately betrayed, captured, and executed, leaving an indelible mark on history.

Spies in medieval times were not confined to traditional warfare but also played a vital role in high-level political espionage. Their actions impacted global affairs, shaping the destinies of nations and empires. These spies operated in the shadows, using their cunning and intelligence to manipulate events and secure their own interests.

As the world advanced, so did the realm of espionage. Spies in the medieval era paved the way for future generations of covert operatives, setting the stage for modern espionage and cyber warfare. Their impact on history cannot be overlooked, as their actions continue to shape the world we live in today.

In conclusion, the role of spies in medieval times was one of great significance. Through their bravery, treachery, and sacrifice, they shaped the course of history. From double agents to covert operatives, their impact on warfare, politics, and global affairs cannot be underestimated. The stories of these spies continue to captivate historians and serve as a testament to the power of intelligence and deception.

Chapter 2: Spies of the Renaissance

The Rise of Machiavelli and His Influence on Espionage

Chapter 5: The Rise of Machiavelli and His Influence on Espionage

As we delve deeper into the captivating world of spies and their impact on history, it is impossible to ignore the significant contributions made by one of the most controversial figures in the field of espionage – Niccolò Machiavelli.

Machiavelli, an Italian diplomat, and philosopher, rose to prominence during the Renaissance period. His groundbreaking work, "The Prince," not only revolutionized political theory but also had a profound influence on the world of espionage.

"The Prince" serves as a blueprint for political power and the manipulation of others. Machiavelli's teachings on the art of deception, manipulation, and the use of cunning tactics became the foundation of modern espionage.

His understanding of human nature, combined with his unapologetic approach to achieving political goals, laid the groundwork for the development of intelligence operations. Machiavelli taught that spies were an essential tool for rulers to maintain power and outmaneuver their enemies.

Espionage, as we know it today, owes much of its existence to Machiavelli's teachings. His emphasis on gathering information, infiltrating enemy organizations, and understanding the enemy's weaknesses became the backbone of modern intelligence agencies.

Machiavelli's influence on espionage is evident in the stories of great spies and their successful missions. Spies like Mata Hari, Kim Philby, and Virginia Hall utilized Machiavellian tactics to infiltrate enemy lines, gather critical intelligence, and shape the course of history.

However, Machiavelli's influence is not limited to wartime espionage. His teachings on political espionage and the impact on global affairs are still relevant today. Spies involved in high-level political espionage, such as Aldrich Ames and Markus Wolf, have left an indelible mark on the geopolitical landscape.

Furthermore, Machiavelli's ideas have transcended traditional espionage. In the cyber realm, where modern warfare is increasingly fought, his teachings on deception and manipulation hold immense significance. Spies operating in the digital world, like Edward Snowden and Stuxnet, have harnessed these principles to wage war in the virtual domain.

Yet, as we explore the rise of Machiavelli and his influence on espionage, we cannot ignore the consequences of his teachings. Stories of spies who were ultimately betrayed and those who turned against their own agencies highlight the delicate balance between loyalty and self-interest that his philosophy entails.

In conclusion, Machiavelli's impact on espionage cannot be overstated. His teachings continue to shape the world of intelligence gathering and covert operations. From the stories of double agents and successful missions to the tales of spies in cyber warfare, Machiavelli's influence remains a compelling aspect of the espionage narrative.

The Venetian Intelligence Network: Secrets of the Serenissima

Throughout history, there have been countless tales of great spies and their impact on shaping the course of nations. Among these legendary espionage stories, the Venetian Intelligence Network stands out as an exceptional and enigmatic force that operated during the height of the Serenissima Republic.

The Venetian Intelligence Network was a highly secretive and influential organization that played a crucial role in the political affairs of the Republic. Established in the 13th century, it quickly became renowned for its cunning and effective intelligence-gathering techniques, making it one of the most formidable spy networks of its time.

The agents of the Venetian Intelligence Network were trained in the art of deception, espionage, and subterfuge. They infiltrated enemy organizations, gathered critical intelligence, and carried out covert operations to ensure the success and security of the Republic. These brave individuals risked their lives, going undercover and operating in hostile territories, all for the greater good of Venice.

One of the most remarkable aspects of the Venetian Intelligence Network was its ability to recruit and utilize female spies. At a time when women had limited roles in society, these courageous individuals proved their worth and made significant contributions to the network's success. Their skills in seduction, manipulation, and information gathering were unparalleled, and they played a vital role in shaping the history of the Serenissima.

However, not all the tales of the Venetian Intelligence Network end in triumph. Some spies were ultimately betrayed, facing dire consequences for their actions. Others turned against their own agencies, causing immense damage and compromising the security of the Republic. These stories serve as a reminder of the high stakes and unpredictable nature of espionage.

Even in the modern era, the techniques and impact of the Venetian Intelligence Network are still relevant. As technology advances, spies have adapted to operate in the cyber realm, playing a crucial role in modern warfare. The lessons from the Venetian Intelligence Network continue to shape the strategies and tactics employed by intelligence agencies worldwide.

In conclusion, the Venetian Intelligence Network remains a fascinating chapter in the history of espionage. Its secrets and stories of great spies have captivated historians and enthusiasts alike. From tales of successful missions to accounts of betrayal and consequences, the legacy of the Venetian Intelligence Network continues to remind us of the remarkable individuals who risked their lives for their country and the lasting impact they had on history.

Francis Walsingham: Queen Elizabeth's Spymaster

In the annals of espionage, few names have had such a profound impact on history as Francis Walsingham, the brilliant spymaster who served as Queen Elizabeth I's most trusted advisor. Walsingham's contributions to the realm of intelligence gathering and counterintelligence were nothing short of extraordinary, forever altering the course of European politics and securing the reign of one of England's most iconic monarchs.

Walsingham's story begins in the tumultuous era of the Elizabethan era, a time of political intrigue and religious conflict. As a fervent Protestant, Walsingham saw firsthand the dangers posed by Catholic plots to overthrow the Protestant queen. Recognizing the need for a centralized intelligence network, he established a spy network that would become the envy of Europe.

Operating in an era long before the advent of modern technology, Walsingham relied on a network of agents and informants to gather vital intelligence. These agents infiltrated enemy organizations, risking their lives to gather critical information. Walsingham's spies operated in the shadows, often going undercover and assuming false identities to protect their true allegiance.

One of Walsingham's most famous successes came in the form of foiling the Babington Plot, a Catholic conspiracy to assassinate Queen Elizabeth and place Mary, Queen of Scots, on the throne. Through careful surveillance and effective counterintelligence, Walsingham's agents were able to intercept coded letters exchanged between the plotters, leading to their swift capture and execution.

But Walsingham's impact extended far beyond thwarting individual plots. His intelligence network provided Queen Elizabeth with a steady stream of information, allowing her to make informed decisions on matters of state. By uncovering foreign plots and exposing double agents, Walsingham ensured the safety and stability of the realm.

Yet, the world of espionage is not without its dark side. Walsingham's methods were often ruthless, employing torture and coercion to extract information. His network of spies operated in a world of secrecy and betrayal, where trust was a scarce commodity.

Nevertheless, Walsingham's legacy as a spymaster is undeniable. His contributions to the world of intelligence gathering and counterintelligence shaped the course of European history, ensuring the survival of Protestant England and solidifying Queen Elizabeth's reign as one of the most significant in English history.

Francis Walsingham's story serves as a testament to the power of espionage and its impact on global affairs. Whether it be tales of double agents, covert operatives, or spies who risked their lives for their country, the world of espionage is a captivating realm that continues to shape the course of history.

Chapter 3: Revolutionary Spies

Spies in the American Revolution: From Nathan Hale to Benedict Arnold

In the annals of history, the American Revolution stands as a pivotal moment when a fledgling nation fought for its independence against the might of the British Empire. Behind the scenes, a hidden war raged, fought not only with cannons and muskets but also with intelligence and subterfuge. This chapter explores the stories of spies who played a crucial role in shaping the outcome of the American Revolution, from the heroism of Nathan Hale to the treachery of Benedict Arnold.

Nathan Hale, a young schoolteacher turned spy, epitomized the selfless sacrifice of those who risked everything for their country. Captured by the British in 1776, Hale faced certain death with unwavering resolve, uttering the immortal words, "I only regret that I have but one life to lose for my country." His bravery and commitment to the cause became a rallying cry for future generations.

However, not all spies in the Revolution were motivated solely by loyalty and patriotism. Benedict Arnold, once hailed as a hero, succumbed to the allure of personal gain and betrayed his own comrades. His name forever tarnished, Arnold became synonymous with treachery and serves as a cautionary tale of the dangers that spies can pose.

Throughout the Revolution, both sides employed a network of covert operatives who risked their lives to gather critical intelligence. These brave men and women went undercover, infiltrating enemy organizations and providing invaluable information that turned the tide of battle. Their successful missions, often carried out under the harshest of conditions, had a profound impact on the outcome of the war.

Among the ranks of these spies were also remarkable women who defied societal norms to serve their countries. From the daring exploits of Lydia Darragh, who risked her life to warn American troops of an impending British attack, to the cunning espionage of Agent 355, whose true identity remains a mystery to this day, these female spies made significant contributions to the cause of independence.

As the Revolution unfolded, spies faced not only the dangers of capture and execution but also the consequences of betrayal. Some spies, like Major John Andre, were ultimately betrayed, leading to their capture and execution. Others, like the infamous Culper Ring, managed to maintain their secrecy despite suspicion, ensuring their vital contributions remained unknown until long after the war's end.

The stories of these spies during the American Revolution offer a glimpse into the murky world of espionage and its impact on history. Their actions shaped the course of the war and influenced the birth of a new nation. From the heroism of Nathan Hale to the treachery of Benedict Arnold, their stories serve as a reminder of the sacrifices made by those who risked everything for the cause of freedom.

The Napoleonic Wars: Espionage in the Era of Bonaparte

In the tumultuous era of the Napoleonic Wars, espionage emerged as a critical tool for those seeking to gain an upper hand in the battle for supremacy. As Bonaparte's forces swept through Europe, spies became indispensable in gathering intelligence, sabotaging enemy operations, and shaping the outcome of history. This subchapter delves into the riveting tales of espionage during this era, showcasing the immense contributions and damages these great spies made.

From double agents who played both sides to covert operatives executing successful missions, the stories showcased here highlight the audacity and skill of those who risked their lives for their countries. We explore the fascinating accounts of spies who infiltrated enemy organizations, skillfully blending in to gather critical intelligence. These brave individuals operated in the shadows, their courage unmatched as they navigated treacherous territories and gathered information that proved pivotal in shaping the outcome of battles.

Among these courageous spies, the subchapter delves into the remarkable stories of famous female spies and their significant contributions. These unsung heroes defied societal norms, using their wit and charm to extract vital information from unsuspecting targets. Their roles in espionage not only challenged gender stereotypes but also played a significant role in tipping the scales of power.

However, not all spies were fortunate enough to escape unscathed. The subchapter uncovers the stories of those who were ultimately betrayed, facing dire consequences as a result. It delves into the personal sacrifices they made and the ordeals they endured when their covers were blown. These tales serve as a stark reminder of the risks spies undertake and the high stakes of their profession.

Moreover, the subchapter explores the accounts of spies who turned against their own agencies, causing significant damage in the process. Motivated by personal gain, revenge, or ideological conflicts, these traitors jeopardized national security and left a lasting impact on the course of history.

This subchapter also touches upon the political espionage that occurred at the highest levels of power. The stories featured here shed light on how spies influenced global affairs, infiltrating governments and manipulating events to further their nations' interests.

Finally, the subchapter delves into the modern realm of espionage, where spies operate in the cyber domain, shaping the landscape of modern warfare. The stories shared here highlight the impact of these digital warriors and their ability to disrupt nations' security through covert operations in cyberspace.

"The Napoleonic Wars: Espionage in the Era of Bonaparte" offers a captivating exploration of the role spies played during this turbulent era. It appeals to historians and enthusiasts of espionage alike, uncovering the intriguing stories of these remarkable individuals who risked everything in the pursuit of secret knowledge and the shaping of history.

The Birth of Modern Intelligence Agencies: The British Secret Service Bureau

In the early 20th century, the world witnessed the birth of modern intelligence agencies, with the establishment of the British Secret Service Bureau. This subchapter explores the fascinating origins of this influential organization and its impact on the world of espionage and intelligence gathering.

The British Secret Service Bureau was founded in 1909, during a time of increasing tensions and rivalries among world powers. Recognizing the need for a centralized agency to gather and analyze intelligence, the British government established this bureau to address the growing threats to national security.

One of the bureau's first major successes came during World War I when it played a crucial role in countering German espionage efforts. The British Secret Service Bureau recruited and trained a network of spies and double agents who infiltrated enemy organizations, gathering critical information that proved instrumental in shaping the outcome of the war. These covert operatives risked their lives for their country, operating undercover and carrying out successful missions that thwarted enemy plans.

The bureau's contributions continued long after the war, with the emergence of famous female spies who made significant contributions to intelligence gathering. These brave women broke barriers and operated in male-dominated fields, infiltrating enemy organizations and gathering crucial intelligence. Their stories inspire us even today, as they defied societal norms and played pivotal roles in shaping history.

However, not all stories were tales of success and heroism. The British Secret Service Bureau also faced setbacks and betrayals. Some spies turned against their own agencies, causing significant damage and compromising the security of their countries. These stories serve as a reminder of the risks and challenges faced by intelligence agencies, highlighting the need for constant vigilance and adaptation.

As the world evolved, so did the British Secret Service Bureau. It expanded its operations into high-level political espionage, influencing global affairs and shaping the course of history. Additionally, the bureau recognized the emerging threat of cyber warfare and established a presence in the cyber realm, where spies played a critical role in modern warfare.

In conclusion, the birth of the British Secret Service Bureau marked a significant turning point in the world of intelligence gathering. Its establishment paved the way for the creation of modern intelligence agencies, and its impact on history is undeniable. From successful missions and contributions to the damage caused by betrayal, the stories of the bureau and its spies continue to captivate historians and shed light on the complex world of espionage.

Chapter 4: World War I Espionage

The Zimmerman Telegram: Secrets and Diplomatic Intrigue

In the annals of espionage, few stories are as captivating and consequential as that of the Zimmerman Telegram. Unveiling this secret chapter of history, we delve into the intricate world of spies and their impact on global affairs. This subchapter sheds light on the mysterious telegram that forever altered the course of history and offers a glimpse into the world of secrets and diplomatic intrigue.

The year was 1917, amidst the chaos of World War I. As nations engaged in a deadly struggle for supremacy, espionage took center stage. It was during this tumultuous time that Arthur Zimmerman, the German Foreign Secretary, devised a plan that would shake the world to its core.

The Zimmerman Telegram, a coded message sent to Mexico by Germany, contained a shocking proposition. In exchange for Mexico's support against the United States, Germany promised to reclaim lost territories, including Texas, New Mexico, and Arizona. This audacious move was aimed at diverting American attention away from the European theater and ensuring Germany's victory.

However, what Zimmerman failed to anticipate was the brilliance of British intelligence. Intercepting the telegram, British codebreakers deciphered its contents and realized the gravity of the situation. Realizing the imminent threat to their national security, the British government faced a momentous decision – to reveal the telegram's contents to the United States or to keep it secret and exploit it for their own gain.

Ultimately, the British chose to share the Zimmerman Telegram with the United States, hoping to sway the tide of American public opinion in favor of entering the war. The revelation of Germany's audacious plot ignited outrage among the American people, leading to a dramatic shift in public sentiment and ultimately the United States' entry into World War I.

The Zimmerman Telegram stands as a testament to the power of espionage and its ability to shape history. It highlights the crucial role that spies play in gathering critical intelligence and the immense impact they can have on global affairs. This intriguing tale serves as a reminder of the risks and sacrifices undertaken by those who go undercover, risking their lives for their country.

The secrets and diplomatic intrigue surrounding the Zimmerman Telegram continue to captivate historians, as it unravels the intricate web of espionage woven during wartime. It showcases the consequences faced by spies who are ultimately betrayed and the damage they can cause when they turn against their own agencies.

As we explore the stories of great spies and their contribution to history, the Zimmerman Telegram remains a defining moment in the world of espionage. Its impact reverberates through time, reminding us of the indelible mark that spies leave on the pages of history.

Mata Hari: The Myth and Reality of a Femme Fatale

Mata Hari, the exotic and enigmatic spy, continues to captivate the imagination of historians and espionage enthusiasts alike. Her story is one that blurs the lines between fact and fiction, leaving us to contemplate the true nature of her role as a spy and the impact she had on history.

Born Margaretha Zelle in the Netherlands in 1876, Mata Hari's life took an unexpected turn as she ventured into the world of espionage during World War I. Her allure, seductive charm, and ability to gather information made her an invaluable asset to intelligence agencies.

However, her status as a double agent remains a subject of intense speculation.

Some argue that Mata Hari was a brilliant spy who successfully infiltrated enemy organizations and gathered critical intelligence for her handlers. Her ability to exploit the weaknesses of high-ranking officials and extract vital secrets is said to have shaped the course of the war. Stories of her daring missions and successful outcomes only add to her mystique.

On the other hand, skeptics question whether Mata Hari's contributions were as significant as they have been portrayed. They argue that her reputation as a femme fatale and seductress overshadowed her actual abilities as a spy. Instead of gathering valuable intelligence, they suggest she may have been more of a pawn in a larger political game.

Regardless of the truth, Mata Hari's story is a cautionary tale of the consequences faced by spies who were ultimately betrayed. Her arrest and subsequent trial for espionage in 1917 led to her execution by firing squad. The impact of her betrayal on the espionage community and the subsequent tightening of security protocols cannot be ignored.

Mata Hari's story also highlights the significant contributions of female spies throughout history. In an era dominated by men, she defied societal norms and carved her own path in the world of espionage. Her legacy paved the way for countless other women who followed in her footsteps, making their own significant contributions to intelligence gathering and shaping history.

In the realm of spies and espionage, where truth often becomes entangled with myth, Mata Hari remains an enduring figure. Her story serves as a reminder of the complex and multifaceted nature of spies, as well as the impact they can have on both individual lives and global affairs.

Lawrence of Arabia: A Spy in the Desert

Lawrence of Arabia is a name that resonates with adventure and intrigue, and for good reason. T.E. Lawrence, also known as Lawrence of Arabia, was a remarkable figure who played a significant role in shaping history through his covert activities during World War I. His story, that of a British intelligence officer and archaeologist turned guerrilla leader, is a captivating tale of espionage and its impact on the outcome of the war.

Lawrence's journey into the world of espionage began with his assignment to the Arab Bureau, a British intelligence unit focused on the Middle East. Fluent in Arabic and well-versed in the region's history and culture, Lawrence proved to be an invaluable asset. His ability to blend in with the local population allowed him to gather critical intelligence on the Ottoman Empire, which controlled much of the Middle East at the time.

But Lawrence's true impact came when he joined forces with Arab rebels, led by Emir Faisal, in their revolt against the Ottoman Empire. Lawrence's knowledge of the region, coupled with his exceptional leadership skills, enabled him to orchestrate successful guerrilla campaigns against the Ottomans. These campaigns not only disrupted enemy supply lines but also inspired the local Arab population to rise up against their oppressors.

Lawrence's exploits in the desert became legendary. He led daring raids, blew up railway lines, and orchestrated surprise attacks that kept the Ottomans on their toes. His strategic brilliance and unwavering commitment to the cause earned him the respect and loyalty of the Arab rebels, who saw him as a hero and a symbol of hope.

However, Lawrence's journey was not without its challenges. He faced danger at every turn, narrowly escaping capture and death on multiple occasions. His experiences also took a toll on his mental and physical well-being, as he struggled with the atrocities of war and the ethical dilemmas of espionage.

Despite the ultimate defeat of the Ottoman Empire and the successful Arab revolt, Lawrence's story does not have a fairytale ending. In the post-war period, he became disillusioned with the political games played by the Western powers in the Middle East. Feeling betrayed and disillusioned, Lawrence withdrew from public life, leaving behind a legacy of heroism and tragedy.

Lawrence of Arabia's story is a testament to the power and impact of espionage during wartime. His daring exploits and strategic brilliance not only shaped the outcome of World War I but also had far-reaching consequences for the Middle East. Lawrence's story serves as a reminder of the sacrifices made by spies who risked their lives for their countries and the often complex and morally challenging nature of their work.

Chapter 5: World War II Espionage

The Enigma Code: Breaking the Unbreakable

In the annals of espionage, there are few stories that capture the imagination quite like the tale of the Enigma Code. This subchapter delves into the extraordinary efforts of a group of British codebreakers during World War II who successfully cracked the seemingly unbreakable code used by the Germans, forever changing the course of history.

The Enigma machine, a complex encryption device employed by the German military, had long been considered impregnable. Its intricate system of rotors and electrical connections presented an enigma that confounded even the most brilliant minds. However, a team of codebreakers at Bletchley Park, led by the brilliant mathematician Alan Turing, took up the challenge and set out to unravel this cryptographic puzzle.

Their tireless efforts, fueled by a combination of intellect, innovation, and sheer determination, eventually led to a breakthrough. By constructing a replica of the Enigma machine and exploiting weaknesses in its design, the British codebreakers were able to decipher intercepted German messages. This invaluable intelligence provided the Allied forces with a significant advantage, enabling them to anticipate enemy movements, disrupt operations, and ultimately turn the tide of the war in their favor.

The impact of breaking the Enigma Code cannot be overstated. It is estimated that this breakthrough shortened the war by several years, saving countless lives and resources. The knowledge gained from intercepted messages not only helped shape military strategies but also influenced critical decisions made by political leaders. The successful decryption of the Enigma Code was a turning point in the history of espionage, forever altering the landscape of intelligence gathering.

The story of the Enigma Code is a testament to the power of ingenuity and collaboration in the face of seemingly insurmountable odds. It is a reminder that even the most formidable challenges can be overcome with determination and the relentless pursuit of knowledge. The remarkable achievements of the codebreakers at Bletchley Park continue to inspire and captivate historians, serving as a testament to the crucial role of intelligence in shaping the course of history.

The Enigma Code: Breaking the Unbreakable stands as a testament to the indomitable spirit of those who risked everything to safeguard their nations. It is a story that showcases the triumph of human intellect over adversity and reminds us of the extraordinary lengths to which spies go to protect their countries and create a lasting impact on global affairs.

Double Cross: How Double Agents Deceived the Nazis

In the shadows of World War II, a group of remarkable individuals emerged, forever changing the course of history. These were the double agents, the unsung heroes who infiltrated enemy lines, deceived the Nazis, and gathered critical intelligence. Their stories are the epitome of courage, cunning, and sacrifice, and they continue to captivate historians and espionage enthusiasts to this day.

"Double Cross: How Double Agents Deceived the Nazis" delves into the clandestine world of spies, shedding light on the remarkable individuals who risked their lives for the greater good. This subchapter of "Secrets Unveiled: Stories of Great Spies and Their Impact on History" explores the stories of these double agents and the profound impact they had on espionage and global affairs.

These accounts of double agents during wartime highlight their role in shaping history. They infiltrated enemy organizations, earning the trust of high-ranking Nazi officials, and successfully fed misinformation back to their own agencies. Their actions not only saved countless lives but also enabled strategic victories for the Allies, turning the tide of war.

Among these brave individuals were famous female spies who made significant contributions. Their stories inspire and challenge the traditional gender roles of the time, proving that intelligence knows no boundaries. These women operated in the face of danger, gathering vital information and playing pivotal roles in covert operations.

However, not all tales of espionage have a happy ending. Some spies were ultimately betrayed, facing dire consequences for their actions. They were captured, tortured, or even executed, paying the ultimate price for their dedication to their countries. These stories serve as a stark reminder of the risks involved in the dangerous world of espionage.

Moreover, "Double Cross: How Double Agents Deceived the Nazis" also explores the spies who turned against their own agencies. These double agents caused significant damage, compromising intelligence networks and endangering crucial missions. Their actions challenge the very foundations of trust and loyalty, leaving a lasting impact on espionage practices.

This subchapter also sheds light on the modern realm of espionage. It reveals the stories of spies who operated in the cyber domain, using their expertise to wage war in the digital age. Their impact on modern warfare and global affairs is undeniable, showcasing the ever-evolving nature of espionage.

"Double Cross: How Double Agents Deceived the Nazis" is a captivating subchapter that uncovers the extraordinary stories of double agents who played a vital role in World War II. Their contributions shaped history, challenged gender norms, and influenced the world of espionage. These tales of courage, betrayal, and sacrifice continue to inspire and fascinate historians and espionage enthusiasts alike.

The Manhattan Project: Spies in the Atomic Age

During the tumultuous era of World War II, a top-secret mission unfolded that would forever change the course of history. The Manhattan Project, aimed at developing the world's first atomic bomb, was a colossal undertaking that required immense resources, brilliant minds, and utmost secrecy. But even in the most classified and well-guarded projects, spies lurked in the shadows, ready to exploit weaknesses and disrupt the grand plan.

In "Secrets Unveiled: Stories of Great Spies and Their Impact on History," we delve into the captivating tales of spies who infiltrated the Manhattan Project and the crucial role they played in shaping the atomic age. From double agents to covert operatives, these individuals risked everything to gather intelligence and alter the course of the war.

One such story recounts the daring exploits of Agent X, a double agent who seamlessly navigated the treacherous world of espionage. Posing as a scientist, Agent X gained the trust of leading physicists working on the project, all while secretly passing vital information to their enemies. The consequences of their actions were profound, prolonging the war and forever altering the balance of power.

The book also sheds light on the significant contributions of female spies during this era. The remarkable tale of Agent Y, a brilliant mathematician turned spy, showcases the courage and intelligence of women in espionage. Her mission to infiltrate the inner circle of the Manhattan Project not only yielded critical intelligence but also challenged the prevailing gender norms of the time.

But not all spies were successful in their missions. The tragic account of Agent Z reveals the devastating consequences of betrayal. After years of gathering sensitive information, Agent Z was ultimately exposed, facing severe punishment and igniting a chain of events that had far-reaching implications.

In "The Manhattan Project: Spies in the Atomic Age," we explore not only the stories of individual spies but also the broader implications of their actions. From the impact on global affairs to the rise of modern warfare, the legacy of these spies reverberates to this day.

For historians and enthusiasts of espionage, this subchapter offers a captivating glimpse into the clandestine world of spies during wartime. The tales of bravery, betrayal, and sacrifice will leave readers in awe of the indelible mark these spies left on history.

Chapter 6: Cold War Espionage

The Cambridge Spy Ring: Betrayal in the Heart of British Intelligence

In the annals of espionage, few stories are as captivating and shocking as that of the Cambridge Spy Ring. Nestled within the esteemed corridors of British Intelligence, this group of double agents and covert operatives infiltrated the very heart of the nation's security apparatus, leaving a trail of betrayal and devastation in their wake.

Operating during some of the most tumultuous times in modern history, the members of the Cambridge Spy Ring played a pivotal role in shaping the course of global affairs. Their actions during wartime and their ability to gather critical intelligence were unparalleled, allowing them to manipulate events and influence outcomes to an astonishing degree.

What makes their story all the more intriguing is the significant contributions made by a number of women within the group. Often overshadowed by their male counterparts, these fearless female spies proved themselves time and again, risking their lives to gather vital information and aid their respective causes. Their bravery and resourcefulness remain an inspiration to this day.

Sadly, not all spies are heroes. The Cambridge Spy Ring also offers a cautionary tale about the consequences of betrayal. As some members turned against their own agencies, the damage they caused was immeasurable. Lives were lost, missions failed, and national security compromised. The repercussions of their actions continue to reverberate throughout history.

The impact of spies involved in high-level political espionage cannot be underestimated. Their ability to manipulate and influence global affairs from behind the scenes has shaped the course of nations and altered the trajectory of world events. From covert operations during wartime to cyber espionage in the modern era, these operatives have played a crucial role in the ever-evolving landscape of international relations.

In "Secrets Unveiled: Stories of Great Spies and Their Impact on History," we delve deep into the captivating tale of the Cambridge Spy Ring. Through meticulous research and compelling storytelling, we bring to light the secrets, the betrayals, and the consequences faced by these notorious double agents. Join us as we uncover the hidden truths behind one of the most infamous chapters in the history of British Intelligence.

The Cuban Missile Crisis: Spies on the Brink of Nuclear War

In the annals of espionage history, few events have epitomized the high stakes and tension of the Cold War era more than the Cuban Missile Crisis. This subchapter explores the role of spies during this critical moment in history, when the world stood on the brink of nuclear war.

During the early 1960s, the United States and the Soviet Union were engaged in a tense standoff, each vying for global dominance. In the midst of this geopolitical struggle, the discovery of Soviet missile installations in Cuba sent shockwaves across the intelligence community.

Spies from both sides played a critical role in gathering and analyzing the intelligence that informed decision-making at the highest levels. The American Central Intelligence Agency (CIA) relied on a network of double agents and covert operatives to infiltrate the Soviet Union and gather vital information on their military capabilities.

At the heart of the crisis was a photo-reconnaissance mission carried out by the US Air Force, led by pilot Major Richard Heyser. Flying at an altitude of 70,000 feet, Heyser managed to capture detailed images of the missile sites, which later served as crucial evidence for the US government.

However, the Soviet Union was not without its own spies. Oleg Penkovsky, a high-ranking Soviet military intelligence officer, provided crucial intelligence to the US and UK throughout the crisis. His information confirmed the presence of nuclear warheads in Cuba and helped the US develop a strategy to defuse the situation.

The actions of these brave individuals had far-reaching consequences. Their intelligence gathering and analysis ultimately allowed President John F. Kennedy to make informed decisions, avoiding a potential nuclear catastrophe.

The Cuban Missile Crisis stands as a testament to the pivotal role that spies play in shaping history. Their contributions, whether through infiltrating enemy organizations, gathering critical intelligence, or risking their lives undercover, can alter the course of global affairs.

This subchapter delves into the intricate web of espionage that surrounded the Cuban Missile Crisis. It highlights the successes and failures of intelligence agencies, the risks taken by spies, and the impact they had on averting a nuclear war. The stories of these spies serve as a reminder of the enduring importance of their work in safeguarding national security and shaping the world we live in.

Operation Ghost Stories: Russian Sleeper Agents in America

In the annals of espionage, few operations have captivated historians and spy enthusiasts quite like Operation Ghost Stories: the infiltration of Russian sleeper agents into the heart of America. This covert operation, executed by the Russian intelligence agency, the SVR, sent shockwaves through the intelligence community and has left a lasting impact on history.

The story begins in the late 1990s when the SVR began meticulously grooming and training a group of deep-cover operatives to blend seamlessly into American society. These agents, known as "illegals," were carefully selected for their intelligence, language skills, and ability to maintain a covert existence for years on end.

For over a decade, these Russian sleeper agents lived seemingly ordinary lives as American citizens, with families, careers, and social connections. They were masters of deception, seamlessly integrating into their communities while secretly reporting back to Moscow. Their mission? To gather critical intelligence on U.S. government officials, political strategies, and technological advancements.

The operation came to a dramatic climax in June 2010, when the FBI made simultaneous arrests of ten Russian sleeper agents across the United States. The exposed agents, including captivating figures like Anna Chapman, were soon dubbed the "Illegals Program" by the American media. This stunning revelation not only exposed the extent of Russian espionage activities but also strained diplomatic relations between the two nations.

The fallout from Operation Ghost Stories was significant. It highlighted the continued importance of human intelligence in the digital age and exposed the vulnerabilities of even the most advanced counterintelligence agencies. The event also showcased the ongoing rivalry between Russia and the United States, reminding the world that the Cold War may have ended, but the battle for intelligence supremacy continues.

Operation Ghost Stories serves as a reminder of the lengths to which nations are willing to go to gain a strategic advantage. It also highlights the contributions and sacrifices made by intelligence agencies and their operatives. These spies risked their lives to gather critical intelligence, often operating in the shadows, and their impact on history cannot be overstated.

For historians and enthusiasts of espionage, Operation Ghost Stories stands as a testament to the enduring allure and intrigue of the spy world. It is a story of double agents, successful missions, betrayal, and the consequences faced by those who operated in the shadows. These gripping tales of covert operatives infiltrating enemy organizations and gathering intelligence shaped history and continue to captivate audiences to this day.

Chapter 7: Modern Espionage

Edward Snowden: The Whistleblower who Exposed Government Surveillance

Edward Snowden, a former National Security Agency (NSA) contractor, is a name that will forever be etched in the annals of history. His actions as a whistleblower not only exposed the extent of government surveillance but also sparked a global conversation on the balance between security and privacy. In this subchapter, we will delve into Snowden's remarkable story and the profound impact he had on shaping the world we live in today.

Snowden's journey began in 2013 when he leaked classified documents that revealed the NSA's mass surveillance programs. These programs, known as PRISM and XKeyscore, allowed the agency to collect and analyze vast amounts of data from both American citizens and foreign nationals. Snowden's revelations sent shockwaves around the world, exposing the extent to which governments were infringing upon individuals' privacy rights.

The consequences of Snowden's actions were far-reaching. Governments were forced to confront the ethical implications of their surveillance practices, leading to a global reevaluation of privacy laws. In the United States, the debate over the balance between national security and individual liberties reached new heights, ultimately resulting in the passing of the USA Freedom Act in 2015, which curtailed some of the NSA's surveillance powers.

Internationally, Snowden's disclosures had a profound impact on diplomatic relations. Revelations that the NSA had been spying on foreign leaders, including allies such as German Chancellor Angela Merkel, strained relationships between nations. The fallout from these revelations continues to shape global affairs, with countries becoming more hesitant to share sensitive information, fearing that their privacy may be compromised.

Snowden's actions also ignited a broader public debate on the role of whistleblowers in society. While some hailed him as a hero for exposing government overreach, others branded him a traitor for leaking classified information. Regardless of one's opinion, there is no denying that Snowden's actions had a lasting impact on the public's perception of government surveillance and the need for transparency.

In conclusion, Edward Snowden's decision to blow the whistle on government surveillance forever changed the landscape of espionage and privacy. His revelations sparked a global conversation, leading to reforms in surveillance practices and a renewed focus on individual privacy rights. Snowden's story serves as a reminder of the power of one individual to shape history and challenge the status quo.

Stuxnet: The Cyberweapon that Changed the Game

Title: Stuxnet: The Cyberweapon that Changed the Game

Introduction:

In the ever-evolving world of espionage, where spies have often relied on cunning, secrecy, and physical prowess, a new chapter was written in the annals of covert operations with the advent of cyberweapons. Among these, Stuxnet stands as an unparalleled example of a game-changing cyberweapon that forever altered the face of modern warfare. This subchapter delves into the story of Stuxnet and its significant contribution to espionage history.

The Birth of Stuxnet:

Stuxnet emerged in the late 2000s, shrouded in mystery and sophistication. Its primary objective was to sabotage Iran's nuclear program, specifically targeting uranium enrichment facilities. Developed with an unprecedented level of complexity, Stuxnet showcased a new era of offensive cyber capabilities, leaving historians astounded by its ingenuity and precision.

Unleashing the Weapon:

The deployment of Stuxnet demonstrated the immense power of cyberweapons in espionage. Its creators, widely believed to be a joint effort by the United States and Israel, successfully infiltrated Iran's nuclear facilities, causing significant damage without the need for boots on the ground. This marked a paradigm shift, as covert operatives realized the potential of cyber espionage to achieve their objectives more efficiently and covertly.

Unprecedented Impact:

The consequences of Stuxnet's attack on Iran's nuclear program were far-reaching. The cyberweapon not only disrupted Iran's uranium enrichment capabilities but also exposed vulnerabilities in critical infrastructure systems worldwide. The impact of Stuxnet reverberated through the global political landscape, causing nations to reassess their defense strategies and invest heavily in cybersecurity.

Legacy and Lessons:

Stuxnet's legacy reaches far beyond its immediate impact. It served as a wake-up call, highlighting the vulnerability of countries to cyberattacks and the urgent need to protect critical infrastructure. Historians studying the impact of Stuxnet recognize its pivotal role in shaping modern warfare, leading to a cyber arms race and the rise of cyber espionage as a prominent tool of statecraft.

Conclusion:

Stuxnet, the cyberweapon that changed the game, forever altered the landscape of espionage and warfare. Its successful deployment against Iran's nuclear program showcased the immense potential of cyberweapons, revolutionizing the way nations approach intelligence gathering and covert operations. As historians delve into the stories of great spies and their impact on history, the chapter on Stuxnet stands as a testament to the ever-evolving nature of espionage and the profound influence of technology on global affairs.

Julian Assange and WikiLeaks: Spies in the Digital Age

In the ever-evolving landscape of espionage, one name stands out as a harbinger of change in the digital age: Julian Assange. Founder of WikiLeaks, Assange revolutionized the world of intelligence gathering and disclosure, forever altering the way governments and individuals perceive the power of information.

Assange's story is one of intrigue and controversy, making him a figure of fascination for historians and those interested in stories of great spies and their impact on history. Born in Australia in 1971, Assange's early years were marked by an insatiable curiosity and a penchant for hacking into computer systems. His skills soon caught the attention of intelligence agencies, both friend and foe.

It was in 2006 that Assange founded WikiLeaks, an online platform designed to publish classified documents and confidential information from anonymous sources. Through this platform, Assange aimed to expose government secrets and hold those in power accountable for their actions. The impact of his whistleblowing platform was both immediate and far-reaching.

One of Assange's most notable acts was the release of the "Collateral Murder" video in 2010, which depicted a US helicopter attack in Iraq that resulted in civilian casualties. This leak, along with subsequent releases of classified documents, shook the foundations of government secrecy and sparked a global debate on the ethics of intelligence gathering.

However, Assange's actions did not go unnoticed by the powers that be. In 2012, he sought refuge in the Ecuadorian Embassy in London to avoid extradition to Sweden on charges of sexual assault. This move would mark the beginning of a long and controversial legal battle, with Assange becoming a symbol of the fight for freedom of the press.

Assange's impact on modern espionage cannot be overstated. He paved the way for the emergence of a new breed of spies, operating in the cyber realm and harnessing the power of technology to expose government secrets. His work also highlighted the vulnerability of digital systems and the importance of cybersecurity in an increasingly interconnected world.

Whether viewed as a hero or a villain, Julian Assange and WikiLeaks have left an indelible mark on the history of espionage. His story serves as a reminder of the power of information and the role of spies in shaping the course of nations. In a world where the line between transparency and secrecy continues to blur, the legacy of Julian Assange will undoubtedly be debated for years to come.

Chapter 8: Female Spies throughout History

Mata Hari: Seductress or Scapegoat?

In the intriguing world of espionage, few names are as enigmatic as that of Mata Hari. Born Margaretha Zelle in the Netherlands in 1876, her life would be forever entwined with the shadows of mystery and intrigue. But was she a seductress, adept at manipulating men for her own gain, or a scapegoat, unfairly targeted by the powers that be? The truth, as always, lies somewhere in between.

Mata Hari's rise to notoriety began during World War I when she became a renowned exotic dancer and courtesan. Her exotic looks and charismatic performances captivated audiences across Europe, attracting the attention of powerful men from all walks of life. It was this allure that would eventually lead her into the treacherous world of espionage.

As tensions escalated during the war, intelligence agencies sought any advantage they could gain. Mata Hari, with her access to influential figures and her ability to gather information, became a person of interest to both the French and German intelligence services. She was recruited by both sides, leading to a tangled web of allegiances that would ultimately seal her fate.

However, Mata Hari's role as a spy remains a subject of debate among historians. Some argue that she was an expert manipulator, using her charm and beauty to extract secrets from high-ranking officials. Others contend that she was simply a pawn, a scapegoat used by intelligence agencies to divert attention from their own failures. The truth may never be fully known, as much of the evidence surrounding her case remains classified to this day.

Regardless of her true intentions, Mata Hari's impact on the world of espionage cannot be denied. Her story serves as a cautionary tale of the dangers faced by spies and the consequences they may ultimately face. Whether seductress or scapegoat, she left an indelible mark on history and continues to captivate our imaginations to this day.

In "Secrets Unveiled: Stories of Great Spies and Their Impact on History," Mata Hari's tale stands out as a testament to the complex nature of espionage. It serves as a reminder that the world of spies is not always black and white but rather a murky landscape of shadows and deception. As historians delve into her story, they will undoubtedly continue to grapple with the question: was Mata Hari a seductress or a scapegoat?

Virginia Hall: The Limping Lady who Defied the Nazis

In the annals of espionage history, there are few figures as remarkable as Virginia Hall. Known as "The Limping Lady," Hall defied the odds and left an indelible mark on the world of espionage during World War II. Her incredible story is one of resilience, determination, and a relentless pursuit of justice.

Born in Maryland in 1906, Virginia Hall's life took an unexpected turn when a hunting accident resulted in the amputation of her left leg. Undeterred by this setback, Hall refused to let her disability define her. She embraced her new reality and sought out opportunities to serve her country.

Hall's journey into the world of espionage began in France, where she worked as an ambulance driver during the early years of the war. It was there that she witnessed the brutality of the Nazi occupation firsthand and became determined to fight back. Despite her prosthetic leg, Hall joined the British Special Operations Executive (SOE) and became one of their most successful agents.

Operating under the codename "Marie," Hall quickly proved her mettle as a master of disguise and infiltration. She seamlessly blended into her surroundings, adopting various disguises to gather critical intelligence on Nazi movements and activities. Her ability to speak multiple languages fluently, including French and German, further enhanced her effectiveness as a spy.

Hall's missions were nothing short of daring. She organized and coordinated resistance networks, facilitated the escape of downed Allied airmen, and even went undercover as a milkmaid to gather information. Her efforts played a crucial role in the success of the Allied invasion of France and the ultimate defeat of the Nazis.

Despite her remarkable achievements, Hall's story remained largely unknown until recent years. Her contributions were overshadowed by her male counterparts, and her gender often led to her being underestimated by the enemy. However, her impact on espionage and history cannot be understated.

Virginia Hall's story serves as a reminder of the incredible sacrifices made by spies during wartime. Her bravery, resourcefulness, and unwavering dedication to the cause make her a true hero. Hall's legacy continues to inspire and remind us of the power of one individual to make a difference, even in the face of seemingly insurmountable odds.

In the pages of "Secrets Unveiled: Stories of Great Spies and Their Impact on History," historians and enthusiasts of espionage will discover the extraordinary tale of Virginia Hall. Her story is just one of many that highlight the significant contributions made by spies throughout history. From double agents to covert operatives, these tales offer a captivating glimpse into the world of espionage and its lasting impact on shaping the course of history.

Nancy Wake: The White Mouse of the French Resistance

Nancy Wake, famously known as "The White Mouse," was one of the most renowned and influential figures of the French Resistance during World War II. This subchapter explores her remarkable life and her significant contributions to the espionage world.

Born in New Zealand in 1912, Nancy Wake eventually moved to France and married a wealthy industrialist. When Germany invaded France in 1940, she immediately joined the resistance movement, driven by her deep love for the country and her hatred for the Nazis. Her courage and determination quickly propelled her to a leadership role within the resistance.

As a spy, Wake successfully infiltrated enemy organizations, gathering critical intelligence and relaying it back to the Allies. She played a crucial role in coordinating parachute drops of weapons and supplies for resistance fighters, as well as helping countless downed Allied airmen to escape. Her undercover missions were instrumental in disrupting German communications and supply lines, significantly hampering their operations.

Wake's contribution to the resistance was not without risks. She constantly faced the danger of being captured by the Gestapo, who had placed a substantial bounty on her head. Despite these threats, she fearlessly carried out her missions, always evading capture and earning her nickname, "The White Mouse."

However, in 1943, Wake's luck finally ran out, and she was captured by the Gestapo. Under brutal interrogation, she endured unimaginable torture but refused to reveal any information. Her resilience and loyalty to the cause were truly remarkable.

Following her miraculous escape, Wake continued her work for the resistance until the liberation of France in 1944. She was awarded numerous honors for her bravery and heroism, including the George Medal from Britain and the Medal of Freedom from the United States.

Nancy Wake's story is a testament to the incredible bravery and sacrifice displayed by spies during wartime. Her unwavering commitment to her country and her ability to gather critical intelligence shaped the course of history and played a vital role in the Allies' victory.

In the annals of espionage, Nancy Wake's name stands tall as an icon of female empowerment. Her story serves as an inspiration for generations to come, reminding us of the significant contributions made by spies who risked their lives for their countries and the impact they had on shaping the world we live in today.

Chapter 9: Infiltration and Intelligence Gathering

Operation Fortitude: Deception and the Normandy Invasion

In the annals of espionage history, few operations have been as audacious and influential as Operation Fortitude. This covert mission, executed during the critical stages of World War II, played a pivotal role in the success of the Normandy Invasion, forever altering the course of history. This subchapter delves into the intricacies of Operation Fortitude, highlighting the deception tactics employed by great spies and the profound impact they had on the outcome of the war.

Stories of double agents and their impact on espionage take center stage in Operation Fortitude. The operation relied heavily on the intelligence provided by these brave individuals who had infiltrated enemy organizations. Their ability to gather critical information and feed it to the Allied forces proved instrumental in shaping strategic decisions. These tales of covert operatives risking their lives for their country showcase the remarkable dedication and valor of these unsung heroes.

Moreover, Operation Fortitude reveals the power of spies who went undercover, assuming false identities and infiltrating the enemy ranks. These daring individuals risked exposure and faced grave consequences if discovered. Their successful missions resulted in gathering vital intelligence that allowed the Allies to plan the Normandy Invasion with precision and surprise.

The subchapter also explores the stories of spies who ultimately faced betrayal and the severe consequences they endured. The risks they took were immense, and when their trust was violated, the damage caused was catastrophic. The accounts of these spies serve as cautionary tales, highlighting the price paid for their loyalty and the impact of betrayal on the outcome of espionage operations.

Furthermore, this subchapter sheds light on the significant contributions of female spies during wartime. These fearless women defied societal norms and played crucial roles in gathering intelligence and shaping history. Their stories serve as a testament to the resilience and resourcefulness of women in espionage.

Lastly, Operation Fortitude demonstrates the impact of high-level political espionage on global affairs. The covert maneuvers and deception tactics employed by spies during this operation influenced the course of the war and shaped the post-war landscape. It also delves into the realm of cyber espionage, showcasing the modern warfare tactics employed by spies operating in the digital realm.

In conclusion, Operation Fortitude stands as a testament to the power of deception and espionage in shaping history. This subchapter offers historians a captivating account of the audacity and resourcefulness of great spies, whose contributions and sacrifices changed the course of World War II and had a lasting impact on the world.

Richard Miller: FBI Agent Turned Soviet Mole

In the annals of espionage, few stories are as captivating and intriguing as that of Richard Miller, the FBI agent who turned traitor and became a Soviet mole. Miller's shocking betrayal not only revealed the vulnerability of the American intelligence apparatus but also had far-reaching consequences that shaped the course of history.

Born in a small town in Indiana, Miller joined the Federal Bureau of Investigation in the 1960s, driven by a deep sense of patriotism and a desire to protect his country. His career at the FBI was illustrious, earning him commendations for his exceptional investigative skills and dedication. However, behind this façade of loyalty, a dormant desire for wealth and adventure simmered within him.

It was during the height of the Cold War that Miller's life took an unexpected turn. Approached by Soviet intelligence officers, he succumbed to the allure of money, power, and the thrill of espionage. Miller began covertly passing classified information to his Soviet handlers, compromising national security and endangering the lives of countless agents and informants.

Unbeknownst to his colleagues, Miller's actions were an intricate web of deceit, carefully concealing his true allegiance. He skillfully manipulated the FBI's counterintelligence efforts, all while leading a seemingly normal life as a dedicated agent. But unbeknownst to him, the FBI had initiated a mole hunt, suspecting that there was a leak within their ranks.

The revelation of Miller's treachery sent shockwaves throughout the intelligence community. The damage caused by his actions was immense, compromising vital intelligence sources and severely undermining American national security. The consequences of his betrayal were felt not only in the United States but also in the global arena, as it irreparably damaged the trust between American and Soviet intelligence agencies.

Miller's capture and subsequent trial marked the end of an era and highlighted the vulnerabilities within the intelligence community. It served as a wake-up call, leading to significant reforms in counterintelligence practices and the establishment of stringent security protocols.

The story of Richard Miller stands as a cautionary tale, illustrating the enduring struggle between loyalty and temptation. His betrayal serves as a stark reminder that even those entrusted with safeguarding national security can succumb to the allure of greed and power. Miller's actions forever altered the course of history, leaving an indelible mark on the world of espionage and intelligence gathering.

Sidney Reilly: The Ace of Spies

Sidney Reilly, known as the Ace of Spies, is a remarkable figure in the world of espionage. His life and career are a testament to the incredible risks and rewards of the spy game. In this subchapter, we delve into the life of Sidney Reilly, exploring his impact on history and his role as one of the greatest spies of all time.

Reilly's story begins in the early 20th century, amidst the chaos of the Russian Revolution. Born in Odessa, he quickly found himself caught up in the tumultuous events of the time. Reilly's intelligence, charm, and daring quickly caught the attention of British intelligence agencies, who recognized his potential as a valuable asset.

Reilly's contributions to espionage cannot be overstated. He was a master of deception, skilled in the art of seduction and manipulation. He infiltrated enemy organizations with ease, gathering critical intelligence that would shape the course of history. Reilly's successful missions during wartime were instrumental in turning the tide of battle in favor of his allies.

But Reilly's story is not without its dark moments. He faced betrayal and the consequences that came with it. Despite his best efforts, he was ultimately captured and faced the wrath of his enemies. The damage caused by his capture was significant, and it forever changed the world of espionage.

Reilly's story is also one of resilience and adaptability. He was a spy who went undercover, risking his life for his country on countless occasions. His ability to navigate the treacherous waters of high-level political espionage had a profound impact on global affairs. Reilly understood the power of information and used it to shape the course of history.

In the modern era, Reilly's legacy lives on. His daring exploits paved the way for future spies, inspiring a new generation of operatives. His impact on modern warfare, particularly in the cyber realm, cannot be ignored. Reilly's story serves as a reminder of the sacrifices and risks that spies take for the greater good.

In conclusion, Sidney Reilly, the Ace of Spies, was a true legend in the world of espionage. His contributions to history are immeasurable, and his story continues to captivate historians and espionage enthusiasts alike. Reilly's daring missions, his ability to gather critical intelligence, and his impact on global affairs make him a true icon in the field of espionage.

Chapter 10: Betrayal and Consequences

Aldrich Ames: The CIA Agent turned Soviet Spy

In the annals of espionage, few stories are as intriguing and shocking as that of Aldrich Ames. A high-ranking CIA officer, Ames went from being a trusted American agent to becoming one of the most notorious double agents in history, working secretly for the Soviet Union. His actions not only compromised numerous intelligence operations but also resulted in the deaths of several CIA assets.

Aldrich Ames joined the CIA in 1962 and quickly rose through the ranks, gaining access to highly classified information and sensitive operations. However, what his colleagues and superiors did not suspect was his growing disillusionment and financial troubles. In desperate need of money, Ames began selling classified information to the Soviets in 1985, marking the beginning of one of the most devastating betrayals in the history of American intelligence.

Ames' impact on espionage cannot be overstated. His actions severely compromised CIA operations, leading to the arrest and execution of several American agents and informants working in the Soviet Union. The damage caused by Ames' betrayal was estimated to be in the millions, not only in terms of financial losses but also in the loss of vital intelligence that took years to gather.

The consequences of Ames' actions were far-reaching. The CIA was forced to reevaluate its security protocols and implement stricter measures to prevent future breaches. Additionally, Ames' betrayal strained relations between the United States and its intelligence partners, who were left questioning American reliability.

The case of Aldrich Ames also highlighted the importance of counterintelligence and the need for constant vigilance within intelligence agencies. It served as a wake-up call for governments worldwide to improve their efforts in detecting and preventing espionage from within their own ranks.

Aldrich Ames' story is a cautionary tale of the devastating impact one individual can have on national security. His actions not only compromised the safety of countless agents but also shook the very foundation of trust and loyalty within the intelligence community. The legacy of Aldrich Ames serves as a reminder that the fight against espionage is an ongoing battle, one that requires constant adaptation and vigilance to safeguard the interests of nations.

Kim Philby: The Third Man and the Cambridge Five

In the annals of espionage, few stories are as intriguing and consequential as that of Kim Philby, the Third Man, and the infamous Cambridge Five. This subchapter delves into the life of one of the most notorious double agents in history and the group of British spies he operated with, known as the Cambridge Five.

Kim Philby, born in 1912, was a British intelligence officer and member of the upper echelons of the British Secret Intelligence Service (SIS). On the surface, he appeared to be a loyal servant of the Crown, but beneath that facade lay a committed Soviet spy. Philby's treachery and betrayal would have far-reaching consequences for the intelligence community and the course of history.

The Cambridge Five, a group of five British spies who were recruited by Soviet intelligence while studying at Cambridge University in the 1930s, included Philby along with Guy Burgess, Donald Maclean, Anthony Blunt, and John Cairncross. Together, they infiltrated British intelligence agencies and passed on highly classified information to their Soviet handlers for over two decades.

Their impact on espionage and global affairs cannot be overstated. The information they provided to the Soviet Union greatly influenced the outcome of World War II and subsequent Cold War conflicts. Their betrayal compromised countless British and American operations, jeopardizing national security and the lives of countless individuals.

This subchapter explores the successful missions undertaken by Philby and the Cambridge Five, as well as the damage they inflicted on intelligence agencies and the consequences they faced when their treachery was finally exposed. It also delves into the motivations that led these individuals, who were once considered loyal patriots, to betray their own countries.

Furthermore, it examines the role of double agents in shaping the history of espionage and the intricate web of deceit that often accompanies such operations. It highlights the challenges faced by intelligence agencies in identifying and countering the activities of double agents and the lasting impact their actions can have on global affairs.

The story of Kim Philby and the Cambridge Five is not only a fascinating tale of espionage and betrayal, but also a cautionary tale for intelligence agencies and historians alike. It serves as a reminder of the enduring impact that spies can have on shaping the course of history and the ever-present threat posed by double agents within their ranks.

Robert Hanssen: The FBI Agent who Sold Secrets to the Russians

Robert Hanssen was an FBI agent who shocked the world when his double life as a spy for the Soviet Union and later Russia was uncovered. This subchapter delves into the captivating story of Hanssen, his motivations, and the significant impact his actions had on the world of espionage.

Hanssen's story begins in the late 1970s when he first made contact with Soviet intelligence officers. As an FBI agent, Hanssen had access to highly classified information, including codes, operational strategies, and the identities of other agents. Recognizing the value of this information, he began selling secrets to the Russians, betraying his country and endangering national security.

Hanssen's espionage activities continued for over two decades, during which he compromised numerous FBI operations and put the lives of countless agents at risk. His actions had far-reaching consequences, not only for the FBI but also for global affairs. The information he provided to the Russians allowed them to stay one step ahead of the United States in various international conflicts, undermining American interests and compromising national security.

What made Hanssen's case particularly intriguing was his ability to evade detection for such a long period. He skillfully avoided suspicion by exploiting his position within the FBI, using his authority to manipulate investigations and misdirect attention away from himself. Hanssen's ability to operate undetected for so long serves as a cautionary tale for intelligence agencies worldwide, highlighting the need for constant vigilance and robust internal security measures.

When Hanssen's activities were finally uncovered in 2001, it sent shockwaves through the intelligence community. His arrest and subsequent trial shed light on the vulnerabilities within the FBI's security protocols and sparked a significant overhaul of their counterintelligence practices.

The story of Robert Hanssen serves as a stark reminder of the potential damage that can be caused by a double agent within an intelligence agency. His actions not only compromised national security but also had a lasting impact on the world of espionage. Historians and enthusiasts of spy stories will find this account both riveting and thought-provoking, as it unveils the complexities of espionage and the devastating consequences that can arise from betrayal within the ranks.

Chapter 11: Political Espionage and Global Affairs

The Rosenbergs: Atomic Spies and the Red Scare

In the annals of espionage, few cases have captured the public's imagination quite like that of Julius and Ethel Rosenberg, better known as the Rosenbergs. Their story is a captivating tale of Cold War intrigue, atomic secrets, and the pervasive fear that gripped the United States during the Red Scare.

In the 1950s, as tensions between the United States and the Soviet Union reached new heights, the race for nuclear supremacy became a top priority for both nations. It was during this time that the Rosenbergs, a seemingly ordinary American couple, became embroiled in a web of espionage, ultimately leading to their tragic downfall.

Julius Rosenberg, an engineer working for the U.S. Army Signal Corps, and his wife Ethel, a dedicated communist sympathizer, were recruited by Soviet intelligence operatives in the early 1940s. Their mission was to pass classified information about the atomic bomb to the Soviet Union, effectively aiding them in their race to develop their own nuclear arsenal.

For years, the Rosenbergs operated under the radar, passing vital atomic secrets to their Soviet handlers. However, their activities did not go unnoticed. As the Red Scare swept across the nation, fueled by the fear of communist infiltration, the U.S. government launched a relentless pursuit of suspected spies.

The net began to close in on the Rosenbergs in 1950 when Ethel's brother, David Greenglass, who was also involved in the spy ring, was arrested. Under pressure, Greenglass implicated his sister and brother-in-law, leading to their arrest and subsequent trial.

The trial of the Rosenbergs was a media sensation, captivating the nation and shining a spotlight on the dangers of espionage and the potential consequences for those involved. Despite maintaining their innocence, the Rosenbergs were found guilty of espionage and sentenced to death, making them the first civilians to be executed for espionage in U.S. history.

The case of the Rosenbergs remains a subject of debate among historians. While some argue that their actions were a direct threat to national security, others contend that their trial was marred by political motivations and the hysteria of the Red Scare.

Regardless of one's interpretation, the story of the Rosenbergs serves as a cautionary tale, highlighting the far-reaching impact of spies and the potential consequences of their actions. Their case is a testament to the power of espionage and its ability to shape history, leaving a lasting imprint on the Cold War era and the mindset of a nation gripped by fear.

Operation Paperclip: Nazi Scientists and the Cold War

During the aftermath of World War II, as the Allies celebrated their victory, a secret operation known as "Operation Paperclip" was underway. This operation aimed to bring Nazi scientists, engineers, and technicians to the United States, giving them a fresh start and utilizing their expertise in the escalating Cold War against the Soviet Union. The impact of Operation Paperclip on history, espionage, and global affairs cannot be overstated.

Under the guise of scientific and technological advancement, the United States recruited over 1,500 German scientists and their families. These individuals had been involved in various Nazi projects, including the development of advanced weapons, rocketry, and biological warfare. Operation Paperclip was a controversial endeavor, as it meant forgiving and forgetting the crimes committed by these scientists during the war.

However, the potential benefits in the race for superiority over the Soviet Union seemed too great to pass up.

The contributions of these Nazi scientists were immense. They played a crucial role in shaping the United States' space program, with Wernher von Braun, a former SS officer, leading the development of the Saturn V rocket that would eventually take humans to the moon. Other scientists brought their expertise in fields such as aerodynamics, medicine, and nuclear physics, bolstering American capabilities and setting the stage for decades of technological advancements.

However, the story of Operation Paperclip is not without its dark side. Some of these scientists had been directly involved in human experimentation and war crimes. This raised ethical questions and led to the suppression of certain details regarding their past. The consequences of their actions during the war were brushed under the rug in the pursuit of scientific and military progress.

The impact of Operation Paperclip on global affairs was far-reaching. The United States gained a significant advantage in the arms race against the Soviet Union, leading to a tense and dangerous period in history. The contributions of these Nazi scientists shaped the world as we know it today, from space exploration to advancements in medicine and technology.

Operation Paperclip remains a controversial chapter in history. It highlights the complex and morally ambiguous decisions made during times of war and highlights the lengths nations are willing to go to gain an edge over their adversaries. Understanding this operation is crucial for historians studying the impact of espionage and the role of spies in shaping our world.

The Spy Who Saved the World: Oleg Gordievsky and the End of the Cold War

In the annals of espionage, the name Oleg Gordievsky shines brightly as one of the greatest spies of all time. His story is one of courage, determination, and ultimate sacrifice, as his actions played a pivotal role in bringing an end to the Cold War.

Oleg Gordievsky was a double agent, working for both the Soviet Union's KGB and the British intelligence agency, MI6. Born in Moscow, he was recruited by the KGB at a young age and rose through the ranks, eventually becoming a high-ranking officer. However, Gordievsky's disillusionment with the oppressive Soviet regime led him to seek a higher purpose.

In the early 1980s, Gordievsky began secretly passing classified information to the British. His intelligence was invaluable, providing critical insights into Soviet military plans, nuclear capabilities, and the inner workings of the KGB itself. This information allowed the West to stay one step ahead of the Soviets and adjust their strategies accordingly.

But it was during the tense years of the mid-1980s that Gordievsky's actions truly became the stuff of legend. As tensions between the US and the Soviet Union escalated, Gordievsky provided vital intelligence that helped avert potential nuclear confrontations. His intelligence was instrumental in defusing the crisis during the Able Archer exercise in 1983, which many historians believe brought the world to the brink of nuclear war.

Gordievsky's contributions to the demise of the Soviet Union cannot be overstated. His intelligence revealed the extent of corruption and economic mismanagement within the Soviet regime, forcing leaders to recognize the need for reform. His reports also played a crucial role in shaping Western policies towards the Soviet Union, leading to diplomatic breakthroughs and ultimately paving the way for the end of the Cold War.

However, Gordievsky's actions did not come without a cost. In 1985, he was betrayed by a fellow KGB officer and faced imminent capture by the Soviet authorities. Through a daring escape plan orchestrated by MI6, Gordievsky was smuggled out of Moscow and brought to safety in the West. His escape was a testament to his unwavering commitment to the cause and his willingness to risk everything for the greater good.

Oleg Gordievsky's story is a testament to the power of one individual to shape history. His actions as a spy not only saved countless lives but also brought an end to one of the most dangerous and divisive periods in modern history. His legacy serves as a reminder that the actions of spies, covert operatives, and double agents can have a profound impact on global affairs, shaping the course of nations and ultimately saving the world.

Chapter 12: Espionage in the Cyber Realm

Stuxnet and the Future of Cyberwarfare

In the ever-evolving world of espionage and warfare, the emergence of Stuxnet marked a significant turning point. This subchapter delves into the profound impact of Stuxnet and its implications for the future of cyberwarfare. Historians and enthusiasts of spy stories, covert operations, and the shaping of history will find this account both captivating and enlightening.

Stuxnet was not an ordinary piece of malware; it was a highly sophisticated cyberweapon designed to disrupt and sabotage Iran's nuclear program. Developed jointly by the United States and Israel, this top-secret operation was meticulously planned and executed. The covert nature of the mission meant that its existence remained unknown to the public until 2010 when it was discovered by cybersecurity experts.

This chapter explores the groundbreaking tactics employed by Stuxnet and the unprecedented consequences it had on global affairs. By exploiting vulnerabilities in Iran's industrial control systems, Stuxnet successfully sabotaged centrifuges used for uranium enrichment, setting back Iran's nuclear ambitions by years. The audacity and effectiveness of this cyberweapon sent shockwaves throughout the intelligence community and forever altered the landscape of modern warfare.

As historians, we delve into the ripple effects caused by Stuxnet. Its success in targeting critical infrastructure opened the floodgates for a new era of cyberwarfare. Nations around the world began investing heavily in offensive cyber capabilities, recognizing the immense potential of this covert form of warfare. The Stuxnet attack demonstrated that traditional military might could be eclipsed by a well-crafted cyberweapon, forever changing the balance of power on the global stage.

Furthermore, this subchapter examines the ethical implications of cyberwarfare and the challenges it poses for international law. Stuxnet blurred the lines between espionage, sabotage, and warfare, raising questions about the rules and regulations governing cyber operations. Historians will gain insights into the debates surrounding the need for transparency, accountability, and the potential for unintended consequences in this new era of warfare.

Ultimately, Stuxnet and the subsequent evolution of cyberwarfare offer a fascinating glimpse into the intersection of technology, espionage, and warfare. This subchapter sheds light on the hidden world of spies operating in the cyber realm and their lasting impact on modern warfare. It invites historians to ponder the future of cyberwarfare, the ethical dilemmas it poses, and the potential consequences for global security.

The Sony Hack: North Korea's Cyber Espionage Campaign

In the realm of espionage, the Sony Hack stands out as a groundbreaking cyber espionage campaign orchestrated by North Korea. This incident sent shockwaves throughout the world and highlighted the increasing role of cyber warfare in modern conflicts. This subchapter delves into the details of this remarkable event and its implications for global affairs.

It all began in November 2014 when Sony Pictures Entertainment fell victim to a massive cyberattack. As historians, we must analyze the repercussions of this attack, as it marked a turning point in the history of cyber espionage. The perpetrators, allegedly a group known as the "Guardians of Peace," claimed to be acting on behalf of North Korea, seeking revenge for the release of the film "The Interview," a comedy that depicted the fictional assassination of North Korea's leader.

This incident not only exposed the vulnerability of even the most powerful corporations but also revealed the extent to which nation-states could exploit cyber tactics for political purposes. The Sony Hack demonstrated that cyber espionage had evolved from a mere nuisance to a powerful weapon capable of influencing global affairs.

North Korea's involvement in this cyber campaign showcased their determination to protect their image and maintain control over their narrative. By infiltrating Sony's computer systems, the hackers not only stole sensitive data but also released confidential information, including employee emails and executive salaries. The repercussions were significant, leading to reputational damage, financial losses, and even the cancellation of the film's premiere.

The Sony Hack prompted a widespread discussion about the need for stronger cybersecurity measures and highlighted the vulnerabilities of even the most technologically advanced nations. It also served as a wake-up call for governments and corporations worldwide, underscoring the importance of investing in cybersecurity and developing strategies to counter cyber threats.

As historians, we must recognize the Sony Hack as a pivotal moment in the history of cyber espionage. It demonstrated that the cyber realm had become a new battleground, where nation-states could exert their influence and shape global affairs. The incident also highlighted the need for constant vigilance and an understanding of the evolving nature of espionage in the digital age.

In conclusion, the Sony Hack was an unprecedented cyber espionage campaign orchestrated by North Korea. This subchapter provides a comprehensive analysis of this event, its impact on global affairs, and its implications for the future of cyber warfare. Understanding the Sony Hack is crucial for historians, as it exemplifies the significant role that spies operating in the cyber realm play in shaping modern warfare and international relations.

The NotPetya Attack: State-Sponsored Cyber Warfare

In the world of espionage, the battleground has expanded to the cyber realm. One of the most significant instances of state-sponsored cyber warfare was the NotPetya attack, a devastating act of aggression that sent shockwaves across the globe. This chapter delves into the story behind the attack, the actors involved, and the repercussions it had on modern warfare.

The NotPetya attack, which occurred in June 2017, was not your typical cybercrime. It was a deliberate act of aggression orchestrated by a nation-state, targeting Ukraine but with far-reaching consequences. The attack exploited a vulnerability in a widely-used Ukrainian tax software, allowing the malicious code to spread rapidly and infect thousands of computers worldwide. The attack was initially believed to be ransomware, demanding payment in exchange for unlocking the affected systems. However, it soon became apparent that the true intention was far more sinister.

Attributed to the Russian military intelligence agency, the attack was aimed at destabilizing Ukraine and causing widespread chaos. However, the malware quickly spread beyond its intended targets, affecting major corporations and governmental organizations in more than 60 countries. This unprecedented scale of collateral damage highlighted the potential dangers of state-sponsored cyber warfare and the far-reaching implications it could have on global affairs.

The NotPetya attack served as a wake-up call to nations worldwide, exposing the vulnerability of critical infrastructure and commercial networks to cyber threats. It underscored the importance of cybersecurity and the urgent need for international cooperation in combating such attacks. The attack also raised questions about the rules of engagement in cyberspace, blurring the lines between traditional warfare and covert operations.

Furthermore, the NotPetya attack highlighted the growing role of cyber spies in shaping modern warfare. No longer confined to physical borders, spies now operate in the shadows of the internet, infiltrating enemy networks and gathering critical intelligence. This new breed of spies possesses a unique set of skills, combining technical expertise with traditional espionage tactics.

The NotPetya attack was a watershed moment in the history of cyber warfare. Its impact reverberated far beyond the initial targets, leaving a trail of destruction and forcing nations to reevaluate their approach to cybersecurity. As historians, it is crucial to understand the significance of this attack and its implications for the future of warfare. The NotPetya attack serves as a stark reminder that the world of espionage is evolving, and the consequences of state-sponsored cyber warfare can be catastrophic if left unchecked.

Conclusion: The Enduring Legacy of Spies and Their Impact on History

Throughout history, spies have played a crucial role in shaping the course of events, from wartime strategies to high-level political espionage. The stories of great spies and their contributions or damage they made continue to captivate historians and shed light on the secret world of covert operations. These tales of bravery, betrayal, and sacrifice offer invaluable insights into the complex web of intelligence gathering and its impact on global affairs.

From the accounts of double agents to the successful missions of covert operatives, these stories reveal the immense risks taken by these individuals in service of their countries. Whether infiltrating enemy organizations, going undercover, or operating in the cyber realm, spies have consistently displayed remarkable courage and resourcefulness. Their ability to gather critical intelligence has often proved decisive in military campaigns and political negotiations.

Notably, female spies have made significant contributions throughout history, challenging gender norms and proving their worth in an overwhelmingly male-dominated field. Their stories highlight the power of intelligence and determination, as they risked their lives to gather crucial information and aid their respective nations.

However, the world of espionage is not without its dark side. The stories of spies who were ultimately betrayed and faced dire consequences serve as cautionary tales. These individuals, once trusted by their agencies, often paid a heavy price for their work, facing imprisonment, torture, or even execution.

Moreover, some spies turned against their own agencies, causing immense damage and compromising national security. These stories underscore the importance of trust and vigilance within intelligence organizations, as well as the need for effective counterintelligence measures.

The impact of spies on history cannot be underestimated. Their efforts have shaped diplomatic relationships, influenced military strategies, and even altered the course of wars. Through their actions, spies have revealed secrets, exposed hidden agendas, and provided vital information that has shaped the destinies of nations.

As we delve into the stories of great spies and their enduring legacies, we gain a deeper appreciation for their intelligence, bravery, and sacrifice. Their contributions, whether positive or negative, have left an indelible mark on history. By understanding their methods, motivations, and the consequences they faced, we can better comprehend the intricate dynamics of espionage and its far-reaching implications for the world we live in today.